Instagram Marketing

Ultimate Social Media Marketing Guide

How to Reach More Instagram Followers for Your Blog, Brand and Business With Step-by-Step Strategies From Target Audience to Monetization

David Croll

Table of Contents

Get an Audio Book for FREE!

Don't have an Audible account?

Sign up and get "Instagram Marketing" audio book for FREE!

https://goo.gl/WaVpL8

Introduction to Instagram

Instagram is a social networking application created for visual sharing. Founded by Kevin Systrom and Mike Krieger in 2010, the application's popularity grew within a short period of time.

The application serves as a platform for mobile users to upload photos and videos of their choice. The images and videos they upload are added to their profile, which are arranged in a three-row grid. Posts uploaded by users are viewed by their followers. If followers like what they see, they double-tap the post. This is Instagram's version of "liking" a post.

In April 2012, the application was acquired by social networking giant, Facebook, for approximately US$1 billion–in cash and stocks. The application has undergone a number of changes that have contributed to the success that it is enjoying today.

Boasting more than 700 million users, with a little over 50% of them being daily active users, the application has long passed being a platform for personal use. Businesses have adopted the platform, hoping to establish their presence and to cultivate an engaged following.

An engaged following is defined as, "having followers who engage with your blog through comments, likes, and private messages." They are active followers who are interested in your content and what you represent. They contribute to the growth of your brand by sharing your content with their followers and referring your blog to people who might not know your content.

The majority of Instagram's users reside in countries outside of the United States. That means businesses will have access to a global audience–for free. Installing Instagram and creating a blog is free of charge, which is a major benefit for businesses. They have now taken to capitalize on the marketing opportunity the application has provided them. This is because the use of social media has given them a chance to grow their reach to potential clients without spending large amounts of money in the process.

We are living in a visual era–people are moved by the things they see. This is why companies pump so much money into budgets for advertising campaigns on posters, billboards and television advertisements. A product is bound to have a stronger impression on someone if it is presented in a visually pleasing–or visually intriguing–way. This is one of the reasons why Instagram has done so well; it has appealed to a desire shared by the majority of people in the world.

Marketing on Instagram, however, and pulling a following, is not something that will provide instant results. It takes time and hard work to cultivate a following that is engaged with your blog. Strategies need to be rolled out in order for one to experience success on the platform. Tactics need to be considered and applied accordingly. That's what this book is about.

This book is here to guide you through practical ways to find the right audience for your blog; ways to trend; growing your followers; and other useful tips.

This book isn't just for business owners. Instagram is an application that accommodates diversity. People have different reasons for promoting and marketing their Instagram blogs.

Business owners seek to use the platform as a means of attracting more customers for their brands.

Freelancers use the platform to promote their work and seek more clients who would be interested in their services.

There are also individuals who use the application to promote a message or their own personal brand.

You fall into at least one of these categories–there's no question about it. This book will be a useful guide for you as you set out to build your Instagram blog and cultivate your brand. You will find this book to be a useful and eye-opening guide that will make your experience on Instagram worthwhile.

Target Audience: How to Find Your People

Before you can locate your target audience, you need to have a detailed idea about what you are trying to achieve. You cannot afford to run on a vague concept. You need to know what you are trying to sell or promote and the reason behind your actions. What is your motive? What are you hoping to achieve with your idea?

A good place to start is finding the niche your Instagram blog will fall under. If you're struggling on this stage—or if you are not sure what kind of Instagram blog to start—take a look at the following examples for some guidance:

Choose Your Niche

Lifestyle

A lifestyle blog on Instagram is a visual representation of the author's everyday life, interests and activities. The blog will be very personalized—since the content comes from your thoughts and your actions. You will typically find quotes the author will relate to or find inspiring; pictures of areas they visited; pictures of their homes and workplaces; and reflections on the activities that went on during their day. Lifestyle blogs are often created to inspire people on ways of living.

The lifestyle blogger's goal is to be seen as a go-to person when a user is trying to make decisions regarding their daily lives.

Advice for Aspiring Lifestyle Bloggers:

Many people tend to assume that the lifestyle niche is the easiest niche to enter. It may appear to be one of the easiest niches to join, but it is also one of the most competitive niches. There are a lot of people who believe that an audience will learn from how they live their lives. You need to find something about your blog that will set you apart from your competitors. You also need to be sincere with your content. Many people are tempted to exaggerate their lifestyles to attract more followers; don't fall into this trap. Be true to who you are—sincerity always sells.

Travel

A travel blog on Instagram is often dedicated to showcasing the different destinations across the globe the author of the blog visits.

Pictures of popular sites and beautiful scenery are common on Travel blogs. A travel blog can also be used to inform the audience about efficient ways to travel to certain destinations.

The blog doesn't have to be based on international destinations. One could start a travel blog that depicts their locality. The blog could be dedicated to giving viewers from different parts of the world an inside look into what the author's town, city or country looks like. It will inspire the audience to consider visiting that place—which should be the goal of the blog in the first place.

The blog could be dedicated to showcasing the sights and scenery of one location in particular. For example, one could set up an Instagram blog dedicated to showcasing the sights in Switzerland, and they will upload high-quality images of the scenes they came across as the traveled across Switzerland.

The purpose of the travel niche is to encourage the audience to travel to the destinations the blog covers.

Advice for Aspiring Travel Bloggers:

You need to have a sense of adventure and an eye for great destinations and locations if you intend on entering this niche. Travel blogging can become strenuous–especially if you plan on traveling and capturing images on your own. On the flip side, this is a niche with a lot of potential for finding sponsors, partners and other commercial deals. Keep this in mind as you plan your work, and also try to find opportunities to partner with travel agencies, airlines and even hotels and other establishments to minimize costs on your side and to also score financial benefits.

Fashion

Fashion is a major niche on Instagram with diverse expressions; these blogs can showcase clothing and accessories from different brands.

A blog could be dedicated to displaying the latest fashion trends; a fashion blog could take a personal approach as well. There are a number of users on Instagram who use their blogs to exhibit their fashion choices. With every photo they upload, they include the details of the clothing and accessories they are wearing–promoting these brands. Fashion bloggers with large followings often end up becoming ambassadors for popular clothing labels

Some fashion blogs are dedicated to showcasing clothing, accessories and trends from one particular brand. Designer labels like Christian Louboutin, Chanel and Louis Vuitton have Instagram blogs where they promote their latest releases and their most popular products.

For someone who is starting a fashion blog from start, it would be advisable to start as a fashion blogger or as someone who is promoting clothing that they have been designing and selling before they joined Instagram. There is a lot of room for creativity in this niche.

Advice for Aspiring Fashion Bloggers:

You need to be attentive to detail; every piece of fashion and color that you include in your content must be able to attract the attention of your audience. You must also realize that you will be competing with major fashion brands and well-known fashion bloggers, if you are considering this niche, you need to have an out-of-the-box idea in order to have a chance at standing out in this niche.

Beauty

Beauty is also a major niche on Instagram. There are many avenues that can be pursued in this field because of how vast the beauty niche is; some are commercial beauty blogs that are dedicated to advertising beauty products from one particular brand or from several brands.

Make-up artists use their Instagram blogs to showcase their skills by posting the work they have done on clients. Some make-up artists use themselves as models, applying their skills on their own faces.

Some artists use this as a way to promote cosmetic products as ambassadors for a particular brand. Skincare practitioners also make use of the platform to promote their products and offer advice on skincare.

Advice for Aspiring Beauty Bloggers:

You need to be knowledgeable of your craft in this field. You are dealing with sensitive areas like skin and people's image–you have to know what you are doing. If you end up giving the wrong kinds of advice, your reputation as a beauty blogger will spoil. You will lose all credibility, and no one will want to take your advice or see what you have to offer. Make sure that your products are 100% legitimate and the advice you give is genuine.

This is also another niche with many commercial opportunities–there are many make-up, skincare and wellness brands that you can partner with if your blog is successful. Keep this in mind while you plan your content and the direction of your blog.

Food

Food blogs are popular with Instagram users–everybody loves a picture of good food.

Restaurants are using Instagram as a platform to exhibit their best creations. This is with the hope that it will attract more customers.

There are individuals who use their Instagram blog to exhibit their culinary skills. Such blogs are usually created with the intent to find clients, employment or to build their brand as a personal chef.

Some people would prefer to use their Instagram blog to display the different dishes they experience at different eateries.

Advise for Aspiring Food Bloggers:

This is an expensive niche because you will need to have funds available for visiting restaurants or sourcing the food you would like to cook. You will need to be creative with your content because this is another niche where you will be up against big-name chefs, well-known food bloggers and established restaurants. You need to bring your A-game for this niche.

These are a few of the many niches on Instagram. But you can find a lot of other niches like sports, news, entertainment, business and economics, etc. Here are some questions you can consider when trying to find the niche that will work for you best.

What are your interests and your passions?

You need to make sure that what you are planning on venturing into is what you really want to do. Setting up anything, be it a project or a business, can be very challenging. You need to be able to have that drive that will push you through.

What problems would you like to solve for other people?

Once you have listed your interests and your passions, you are able to narrow them down according to which ones will help you solve problems people may have. The blogs that people are able to relate to the most are the ones that are able to meet a need in one way or another. Find how your interests, or your passions, can meet someone's needs.

Who is your competition?

There will be blogs that have similar ideas to the ones you have. It would be good for you to research those who are prominent in the niche you wish to go into. There are tips and pointers you can use whilst setting up your own blog. It's also good to see what you are up against and how your blog can be different.

Is This Idea Profitable?

Does your idea truly have the potential to attract people who will be invested in what you have to offer? If the answer is not a certain yes, or if it is something you cannot work on, you need to re-examine your list and work on it. There is no point in putting your energy into something that has a high chance of not bringing in the results that you want. Go back to the drawing board and work on your idea again.

It is important you know which niche your blog falls under. Otherwise, you will end up generating content that will not attract your desired audience. Knowing your niche will be the first step to deciding on the type of content you will share on your Instagram blog.

Knowing your niche will be the first step to finding your target audience. It helps to have pen and paper with you as we go through this exercise so you can apply it to your own blog.

Target Audience Exercise

Consider the following questions and answer them on your piece of paper.

- **Is your blog directed at people from a specific geographic location?**

If yes, where? If no, think about the regions you would like to target.

- **Is your blog directed at a particular gender or nationality? Is your blog for a certain class of people (working-class, upper-class, etc.)?**

If yes, answer accordingly. If no, take a time to think of who would benefit from your blog the most.

- **Is your blog specific to a particular set of people?**

  For example, if your food blog is for vegetarians then that means that it is only specific to a particular set of people. This question simply means you need to see if your blog is for a large set of people or if it is for a certain group of people with one common interest that a general audience does not share.

- **What age group are you hoping to reach?** Think of those who would find your content or product relevant to their lives.

- **Is your blog designed to educate, entertain or inform?** This question is self-explanatory, but it will help you understand what you are expecting from your target audience.

- **What is your desired outcome for your audience?** What do you want to achieve with your blog? What reaction do you hope to receive from your audience?

These questions will help you narrow down your audience in your niche until you've found your target audience.

Now, you have your target audience, and you have to move to the next step which is planning the content you will generate. An ill-advised decision would be trying to generate content as you go–without planning. If you end up encountering a period where you won't have time to work on the content, in that moment, your blog will suffer.

Plan in advance. That is the best thing you can do for yourself, and it will keep you a step ahead. In a later chapter, we will show you a number of applications you can use to schedule your Instagram posts effectively. You need to plan your content post-by-post. Every post needs careful planning and structuring because every post has the potential to reach more viewers and evoke engagement from your followers.

Find reliable sources for your images. If you are going to use stock images, make sure you subscribe to the right platforms in advance. Collect the photos ahead of time if you can–and make sure they are the best quality that they can possibly be.

If you are going to source your own images through capturing the photos yourself, make sure you schedule a time to take the photos. Plan the locations and call the models you will need in plenty of time.

Make sure that you structure every photoshoot appropriately. Always keep in mind that you are creating content for your target audience. There may be things that you will find appealing that your target audience will not. This is not about what you like or what you do not like. It is about what your target audience is interested in. You need to fulfill their needs and/or their desires in order for them to engage with your blog. You need to remember that you have to give them a reason to return to your blog on a frequent basis.

Make use of the features Instagram has provided. Make use of hashtags–appropriately. We will cover more of this in a later chapter. Instagram recently rolled out the Instagram Stories feature which provided another opportunity for users to showcase their content and to engage with their followers on a more personal level.

You cannot afford to neglect any of the features on Instagram. All of them are able to play an integral part in establishing your presence on the platform.

In the next chapter, we will discuss ways to ensure that your content is as effective as possible.

Effective Content: How to Be in Trend

After the previous chapter, you should have a good understanding about your niche, your target audience, and the kind of content you should be posting on your Instagram blog. The content you will share on Instagram will be displayed through pictures and videos.

Your content cannot be comprised of generic images and videos that hold no particular relevance to your blog or what it represents.

Your content has to be the following:

Relatable

The audience needs to be able to connect with the content on your blog. Relatability is important. People will not feel the need to follow something they cannot relate to or connect with.

Relevant

Your content cannot be outdated. Your posts need to be related to one another. Randomly posting images or videos that have no correlation will confuse your audience. They will not be convinced by what you are claiming to offer.

Informative

Your audience needs to be able to gain something from your blog. You need to strike a balance between posting appealing images and/or videos, and information that the audience will need. Information will often be found in the captions of the images.

Eye-Catching/Aesthetically Pleasing

Remember that Instagram is a visual platform. It's all about the images. You need to make sure that your photos are high quality and are as original as possible. Try to avoid copying other people's photos–the last thing you need are legal issues over something that could be avoided. Put in the work required to produce creative and original posts for your audience to enjoy.

You need to have a target audience in mind before you can create the content for your blog. You cannot expect to reach out to every single user on Instagram. That is neither realistic or practical. There are too many users with different interests and preferences for you to try and harness all of them in. Find the audience that will see what you have to offer as useful and beneficial. There are people on the platform who will be interested in your blog.

Why Content Needs to Be Effective

Now that you have established what kind of content you would like to have on your blog, you need to focus on the next thing– making sure that your content is effective.

How will you know if your content is effective? Content that results in engagement is content that will be considered effective. The main goal of your content should be to evoke a reaction from your followers.

Followers should feel compelled to view more of your content and see more of what you have to offer. Followers should feel compelled to share your content with their followers. They should feel that your content is unique, and they cannot find it anywhere else. Your followers need to feel that they need more of your content after you have posted. First-time visitors should be able to go through your Instagram blog and be impressed with what they see.

First impressions are everything on Instagram. People do not have long attention spans when it comes to social media. If your blog does not leave a good impression on a first-time visitor after they have viewed your content, it will be hard for them to return to your blog. You need to keep this at the back of your mind whenever you are planning your content. Don't just create content to keep your followers interested or engaged. Create content for first-time viewers as well. Your content needs to be good enough to draw them in.

For example, if you are a lifestyle blogger your followers should feel that your blog is the best blog to gain tips on how to navigate through everyday life.

The photos you upload of your daily activities need to be interesting. Don't just upload a photo of you driving to the store. You could upload a photo of the items you brought from the store instead and use that as an opportunity to offer advice on the best products to buy for different things–breakfast, cleaning, etc. Let the backdrop of your photos be attractive. You could upload photos of yourself that were taken in flower gardens or close to a nicely-painted house. These things will boost the aesthetics of your images, and it will also appeal to your followers' visual senses–which is something you cannot afford to neglect.

The quotes and reflections you share on your blog need to be relatable to your audience. This isn't just advice for lifestyle bloggers. Quotes and reflections can appear on Instagram blogs from different niches. When you understand your target audience, you will know what kind of quotes and reflections to share. If your Instagram blog is for teenagers and young adults, you should know that the quotes and reflections you share should relate to the typical issues millennials deal with in their lives–identity, love, friendships, navigating through high school or college, etc.

Millennials are the major target audience for many brands because they are the major generation that is actively on social media. Millennials are the driving force for many advertising campaigns and marketing strategies because businesses and brands have realized that once they are able to harness the attention of millennials, they have secured a reliable consumer group. If your blog is able to attract a follower group that is comprised mainly of the millennial generation, you have made a major step towards success on Instagram. Studies show that a lot of activity on social media–comments, likes and sharing–is done by people from the millennial generation. Millennials are interested in what relates to them and what caters to their needs more than any other generation.

So, why does content need to be effective? When you post content that your followers can relate with directly it gives them the feeling that you care about what they are going through in their lives. They will feel like they connect with your blog on a personal and more emotional level. Having such strong connections with your followers will make them loyal to you, and they will put an effort into making sure that other users on Instagram know about your blog.

You can take this a step further and design your own quotes. Take some time to write them out, and find ones you feel will resonate with your audience. When your followers share the quotes, they will reference you, which will attract more people to come and see what you and your blog are all about.

Keep an Eye on Your Competitors

In the previous chapter, we noted that you need to make sure that you are aware of your competition on Instagram. There are a number of users, with similar ideas to yours, who are trying to tap into the same audience you are trying to attract to your blog. You don't just need to know who your competition is, you need to know what they do, how they do what they do, and how it measures up in comparison to what you are trying to do.

Take notes on the different strategies your competitors have adopted, and see if you can run something similar on your blog. *Do not copy their work idea for idea.* You should use your competitor's blogs as inspiration to do better.

You do not need to view your competitors as 'the enemy." That will lead to breeding unnecessary negativity. Healthy competition is good for any business. It keeps you on your toes and prevents you from slacking. Viewing your competition in an unhealthy light will also lead to making dishonest decisions. You should never consider resorting to underhanded methods like:

Copying your competitor's strategy bit for bit. The one who will be hurt at the end will be you. Once your followers pick up that you are trying to imitate someone else they will lose confidence in you. People can pick up on unoriginal content from a distance. If viewers see that you have nothing of your own to offer, they will leave your blog and focus on your competitor's blog instead since they'll be the ones producing original content.

Measuring your progress against your competitor's success. If you are new to the scene in your niche and you start comparing your progress to your competitor's progress you are going to end up hindering your own progress. When studying your competition, you need to realize that what they do does not reflect on you. It does not speak to the value of your blog. If you notice that you are not doing well in comparison to some of the other blogs that are similar to yours, don't get discouraged. Go back to the drawing board, and formulate more ideas for your blog. You will end up finding methods that will work for you and build your progress. Remember that it's not about how well you do against your competitors. It's about how well you do for *your* blog and your followers. That is what matters.

Running a smear campaign against your competitor. This is downright immature and uncalled for. If you try to build your blog at the expense of your competitor's reputation, you will lose all integrity. Using your blog to speak about your competitor's shortcomings, or trying to show your followers the negative aspects of your competitor's blog, will backfire in the end. If you focus on doing things like this, you will end up forgetting what you're initially meant to be doing–giving your followers good content. You won't be providing good content if the majority of your blog is filled with a hate campaign against your competitors. It will paint *you* in a bad light, and you will actually end up losing credibility with your followers. Don't go down this path. It will not end well.

What Is Your Star Factor and How to Identify It

Originality is a key; we have established this time and time again. One of the best ways to remain original on Instagram is to cultivate your blog in such a way it speaks, "This is what this blog is all about."

You have to have a star factor–something that is unique to your blog. This is your trademark. It has to be something that your competitors do not have–and will have to work extremely hard to get. You cannot afford to accommodate anything generic or unoriginal on your blog. Originality has to be the goal from the get-go.

In order to stand out, your content needs to have something that sets you apart from your other competitors. This is actually something you should have thought of when you were planning your blog.

For example, if you are a photographer, and you are setting up a blog that will showcase your work, you need to make sure that all of your posts have a signature effect or trademark that is unique to your work. You could incorporate a symbolic object like an apple into your photos. No matter the subject, every photo will have an apple strategically positioned in it. This will spark curiosity in your audience, and every time you upload, they will be eager to see how you've managed to incorporate an apple into the image. The object could be anything. Your trademark doesn't even have to be an apple.

27

But it needs to be a particular skill, trick or item that will end up becoming a part of your brand in the long-term.

When people think of McDonald's they think of Big Macs, McNuggets, Happy Meals and Ronald McDonald. McDonald's trademark revolves around its name and the concept of it being a happy place to be. McDonald's competitors have never been able to copy their style, regardless.

In the fashion world, designer label Christian Louboutin is known for red-soled shoes. Every shoe, be it for men, women or children, has a red sole. If the label's competitors try to adopt the red sole, buyers will know that they are trying to imitate the original brand—which will hurt business for the competitors.

In the automobile sphere, Mercedes Benz has a particular style that is unique to the brand. No matter the line of car, people are always able to identify a Mercedes Benz because of their trademark structures and interior. A couple of the brand's competitors landed into serious trouble when they tried imitating Mercedes Benz.

Let your content follow the same line as the mentioned examples. Cultivate a trademark that cannot be copied.

Ways to Identify Your Star Factor

Find what you are really good at doing and capitalize on it. For example, if you are good at manipulating photos, focus on uploading manipulated photos you captured. You can post the original and the edited version of the photo. This will wow your audience, and they will eagerly anticipate what you have to offer next. Let photo manipulation be your selling point in the graphic design niche. Focus on it, and let people know you for that.

If you are selling a line of products on your blog, find the product that you believe will capture the audience's attention, and focus on marketing that product.

For example, if you have a beauty blog that is dedicated to selling skincare products, find the one product you believe will meet the majority of your audience's needs. If your products are for working class women over the age of 30, your star product could be anti-aging that is made from a special ingredient. Focus on marketing that product as the solution to your audience's problems. Women over the age of 30 become very concerned about their face and the lines that develop on their skin. By focusing on promoting a product that will solve their problems, you are generating attention towards your brand and your followers–and customers–will end up believing that your anti-aging cream, and your other products, are the only ones that will work for them.

Promote your blog in a way that makes your followers feel like you are above the rest. Confidence is key in every aspect of life. If you want people to believe in what you have to offer, make them believe it. Make them feel like they are missing out if they do not follow your blog. You have to be wary of becoming overly promotional, though. People may end up thinking your blog is spam if you keep on fueling posts that lack personality and focus solely on promotion.

Allow yourself to brag about your blog a little. If you are a lifestyle blogger, make them feel like your life is amazing. If you are a fashion blogger, make them feel like you are the next editor-in-chief of *Vogue.* If you are offering services, make your followers feel like you are the best one to offer such services—no matter what the service may be.

Sell yourself. Be confident about your blog, and let your followers know it.

People are attracted to confidence. It gives them the sense that you know what you are doing, and they want to learn from you.

If you are the kind of person who struggles with confidence, take some time to build it up. If you have any intention of seeing your Instagram blog be the best one in your niche, you have to be confident in what you do. When you need to take risks and try new things, they will only work if you are confident about them. Otherwise, you will end up failing to reach your desired results.

Use positive and assertive words when captioning your images. When you interact with your followers, be certain of what you say. Let them know that you know what you are doing.

Importance of Content Quality

Content quality is something you cannot afford to neglect or fall short on. Instagram is all about the visuals. Your followers are interested in seeing visuals that will impress them, visuals that will have them talking and wanting to see more. If you are posting low-grade images that you found online, you are selling yourself short.

Followers will not take you seriously if they see that your posts are of a terribly low quality. Do not lift images from Google

Image search and upload them to your blog and expect your followers to be impressed–especially if the images are grainy or if they have watermarks all over them. Your followers will get the impression that you are not serious about what you are doing.

If you are uploading images of your products, don't just post a photo of the product carelessly laid out on any surface. Arrange the product on an attractive surface and make sure everything is uniform or symmetrical. Don't be lazy with the design of your posts.

If you are uploading quotes, let them be on a template that is originally designed and aesthetically pleasing. If you don't know how to create your own templates from scratch, you can enlist the help of a designer who can do it for you, or you can search for an app that will provide you with templates you can use.

If you are going to use stock images for your Instagram blog, search for pictures that are high definition. Most stock sites offer images that are high quality, but you still need to be careful. When you are viewing potential images you'd like to upload, view them in full size to ensure that they aren't grainy or pixelated.

If you are using a stock site for free images, make sure that the watermark on the images does not interfere with them. Do not remove the watermarks without the permission of the owner of the images. Do not use commercial images without the owner's permission. You could be sued if you do such a thing.

High quality images increase the visual experience for your audience. Photographs that have been constructed with care will also contribute to the aesthetics of your blog. You need to pay attention to detail when it comes to running an Instagram blog.

Your followers need to see that you do pay attention to detail. It will build their confidence in your blog.

Mistakes That Should Be Avoided

Take note of the few things you should avoid doing in order to prevent yourself from making major mistakes.

Don't be overly promotional.

If your feed is filled with promotional content, your followers will get more of a 'spam' vibe from your blog. No one likes spam. If your followers feel a disconnect with your blog, they may cease to engage with your posts. Some of your followers might end up unfollowing. Strike a balance between promoting your blog and actively engaging with your followers.

Don't ignore the response/feedback you receive from followers. You should also actively seek feedback from your followers. You could send them a questionnaire, or engage them in actual conversation, to understand what they truly think of your blog. The response you receive from them could help you tweak the areas you aren't performing well in, and capitalize on the areas you are doing well in.

Do not neglect captions. Try to avoid uploading images without captions. Captions help your followers gain more insight on the image you have uploaded. Captions are also what you will use to engage with your followers. The right kinds of captions give your followers the context of your posts, and they can also contribute to evoking a response from your viewers. You could pose a question in the caption which will encourage followers to comment with an answer. Don't make your captions too long. 200 characters should be more than enough to pass a message along. Make use of emojis as well. They make your posts more personal and lively. Every smartphone comes with a range of emojis you can use. Add them to your posts as well.

Don't neglect your community. Some people tend to make the mistake of thinking that their Instagram blog is a one-way thing. They ignore their followers' comments and messages. Doing so never plays out well. Your followers will end up getting the impression that you are not interested in what they have to say, and they will jump ship. They will end up paying more attention to a blog, which would most probably be one of your competitors, that hears them out and cares about their voice.

Don't just wait for your followers to reach out to you. Reach out to them. You could make a habit of contacting a handful of followers every week, to appreciate them for following your content and supporting them. They are, after all, the reason your blog is up and running. A blog without engaging followers will not be successful.

Do not underutilize the application. Make use of the Instagram stories. Make use of hashtags. Use your inbox to communicate with your followers and collaborators. Don't just rely on uploading photos. Use the different features that the application has provided. Link your Instagram blog to your Facebook blog if you have one. This will also increase your reach. Instagram recently rolled out a feature that allows you to upload multiple photos as one post. Make use of that. You could use the feature to tell a story through a series of photos. You could also use the feature to showcase a range of new products. Don't be lazy. The more features you use, the more content you are generating.

Instagram For Business: How to Build Your Brand on Instagram

You need to see your business, initiative or project as a brand.

You need to see it as something that is marketable and something the world needs to see and invest in. In the previous chapter, the importance of confidence was something that was spoken about. You need to take your venturing into Instagram as seriously as possible. When you take something seriously, you will be compelled to put all of your effort into it. That's how you should see your blog because that is what it is. You have a brand, and in order for it to be successful, it needs to have a noticeable impact on the Instagram community. In order for this to happen, you need to build on your brand. What does that mean? It means that you will take to developing your business from a personal and business point of view. By constantly raising awareness of your brand and what you have to offer, you are building your brand. You can make use of campaign tactics and strategies to increase awareness of your brand. Many of the tips and pointers in the previous chapter will contribute to building your brand through the content you post.

This chapter has provided profiles on a couple of the most successful brands on Instagram. In these profiles, you will find information on what these brands do, the reasons behind their success and what you can learn from them so your brand can be successful on Instagram, too.

One thing you will notice about these brands is that their respective niches are either highly competitive or challenging when it comes to finding a target audience. But they've taken such curveballs, and they have made them work in their favor.

None of these brands are the first to do what they do, but they've managed to carve their own path in their respective niches. This is no easy feat. You will find that ,as you go through their profiles, you will be inspired or moved to do more for your brand. You will get a better understanding about building your brand on Instagram and seeing your blog as a business—regardless of what the blog may be about.

If your blog belongs to a niche that is highly saturated, or a niche that has a target audience that may not be easy to tap into, you will find ways to navigate through these changes, and who knows, maybe someone will use your brand as an example for successful brands on Instagram.

Examples of Real Cases

Califia Farms (@califiafarms)

Who Are They?

Califia Farms is a brand known for producing and selling beverages that are made from natural ingredients. Their beverage products range from coffees to milk and juices. The beverages are bottled in uniquely-shaped, and creatively designed, packaging. Califia Farms received top honors in the global packaging design category from the *Beverage World Magazine* awards. This brand was also recognized as one of the most successful brands on Instagram by top Internet Marketing Company HubSpot.

Califia Farms uses Instagram to showcase their innovatively-designed and eye-catching packaging. The brand has amassed just under 70,000 followers on Instagram, with a significant amount of them engaging with the blog on a regular basis.

Why Are They Successful?

You can tell that Califia Farms' success is not accidental. There are tactics and strategies that they applied in order to harness their audience and gain the success they have achieved. Their strategies required a great amount of thinking and planning. These are the major aspects they focused and worked on in order to appeal to their target audience and build their brand:

Their content is aesthetically pleasing. It appeals to the viewers' senses. Califia Farms' Instagram blog is known for having beautiful, high quality images. Every image is strategically curated and captured. Whether the bottle is the focal point of the image or if it serves as an accessory in the image, the beverage product is depicted in a context that is appealing to the brand's target audience: physically active users who are seeking to maintain a healthy lifestyle. Califia Farms has managed to strike a balance between posting relatable content and promoting their product at the same time. Viewers don't feel like they are being overwhelmed with spam-like content.

Every Califia Farms product is captured against a simple backdrop—be it indoors or outdoors. Typical backgrounds you'll find in their images are countertop surfaces, aisles in stores, or natural, green backgrounds. Their posts are visually consistent–they unify one another.

One takes pleasure in perusing the Califia Farms blog on Instagram because they know that their eyes are in for a treat. The brand also makes use of innovative creative concepts in their photos; every post contains a different concept or idea. Every post gives one a sense of enjoyment and activity–they make the viewer want to be active and indulge in the beverages.

When someone looks at a post uploaded by Califia Farms, they aren't just satisfied visually. The posts have a way of appealing to your sense of taste and sense of smell. You will feel like eating or drinking what is displayed in the content. You will feel as if you can smell the flavors of the beverage in the image.

When you look at every post, you can tell that time and care were taken to create the images. The product wasn't just carelessly placed against a backdrop. They make use of design concepts such as lighting, symmetry and value to ensure that their content is a design dream. The Califia Farms Instagram blog exudes originality because that is exactly what their content is–original. You can tell that their ideas are their own.

Their content is lively. The brand isn't just known for uploading images that are attractive or appealing. Videos and GIFs can be found on the blog as well. These are part of the brand's trademark and their overall message which is about being healthy and being active. They depict this through videos and GIFs that are lively and playful in nature. The brand often uses videos as a means to teach their followers how to make certain products—like steaming non-dairy milk, for example. Instead of loading the videos with information that could come across as boring, Califia Farms makes their videos fun and interactive—which results in engagement with followers. The videos are also curated carefully in order to pass the main message whilst appealing to the followers' visual senses. You can tell that they took time to plan the videos in order to execute them perfectly.

The use of videos and GIFs gives the blog an active vibe. It is also a nifty way of diversifying the kind of content they give their followers. Instead of continuously uploading static images, they went the extra mile to ensure that their content expresses the fun and active agenda they are trying to pass.

Sometimes they upload videos for the sole purpose of entertaining their followers. The videos won't contain any tangible information the followers need to capture, but the videos sure are fun to watch.

Keeping content diverse keeps followers entertained and eagerly anticipating what's going to come next. When you ask a follower about the brand, they will be able to give you a clear description of what the brand is about. This is because of the brand's consistency and creativity when it comes to the content they upload.

They make good use of their captions. Califia Farms' creativity overflows into the captions they add to the images, videos and GIFs they upload. Captions are an important part of an Instagram blog, and this brand definitely did not neglect that. They've used their captions to their advantage as well. Every caption is specific to the post it accompanies.

Since they know that the majority of their followers are under the age of 30, the colloquialisms used in the captions and the style in which the captions are written give the captions a youthful vibe. They address the audience in their captions as if they are talking to their friends–which allows the audience to connect with the brand on a personal level.

The captions are also specific to the post they accompany. Every caption includes the appropriate hashtags and the text included in the captions are relative to the image. There is harmony between the image, video, or GIF and the caption – which is something many brands tend to overlook when uploading content.

They make use of emojis which is a major plus. Social media is all about the emojis, and when they are used appropriately, they can boost the post. Emojis also make the captions livelier.

Their captions, like their posts, are also simple. They do not add unnecessary information or text. Unless it's a dedication or special announcement, Califia Farms' captions are usually short and witty in nature. It takes skill to be able to come up with captions like that. This works for them because followers often respond to the images and the captions.

Their content is relatable. It's clear that Califia Farms has a following that engages in what they upload. Every post has comments underneath them. The comments are often in response to what has been posted.

Califia Farms doesn't upload content that does not relate to their brand or their target audience. As mentioned earlier, they don't just upload monotonous images of their product. They are creative with their advertising

Califia Farms hasn't used their knowledge of their target audience to exploit their interests or overload them with content. The content on Califia Farms' Instagram blog is tailored to connect with followers and first-time viewers on a personal level.

Most of the images are set in locations that are part of people's everyday lives. They place their products on countertops, in supermarkets, at picnics, in workout spaces and on kitchen tables. These are areas that are typical to their target audience. When their followers view their content, they get the impression that the brand understands them and truly cares about their needs. The brand also makes use of young models, who are often kitted out in athletic or casual gear, in their images and videos. This is a reflection of their target audience. When their followers see the models in Califia Farms' posts, they see themselves–they see people they can relate to.

All of this creates a personal connection with their audience. The audience feels like they can depend on the brand because of the care the brand took to make the audience feel represented. When a brand is able to cultivate a following that connects with them and feels loyal to the brand, it is only a matter of time before the brand experiences constant growth.

What Can You Learn from Them?

There is power in simplicity. Often, people make the mistake of thinking that their posts have to have complex designs and a lot of color in order to catch the attention of the audience. Relying on a method like this can actual repel your audience instead of attracting them. When brands focus on unnecessary complications, the structure and nature of the posts are often neglected. For example, if you upload a post with text and a background that is filled with colorful vectors and many brightly-colored streaks, your followers might not be able to decipher the actual message you are trying to pass through the post. Take a look at what is essential for the post, and find simple ways to enhance them. Make use of backgrounds that complement the focal point of your post. Avoid bright colors that can clash with the focal point of your image, unless you are trying to go with a psychedelic theme. You can add accessories to the product if that is what you are trying to capture in order to liven the scene. Position everything in your images, and make sure the image is balanced. Try not to do too much. You may end up missing the mark instead of hitting it. If you are searching for images to use, look for images that are visually balanced. Avoid images that have clashing colors and objects that do not relate to one another.

Know your target audience, and use this knowledge to help you engage with the audience. The mistake many brands make is to gain a full understanding of their audience in order to manipulate them into investing in their brand. Some brands have no care about their target audience, and this always backfires on them. Remember that you are dealing with people who have minds of their own. It is you who needs them. Without the audience, you will have no following, and your blog will be irrelevant. See it as trying to get to know someone better so you can become their friend. Envision your followers as your friends. Engage with them through your captions and through the posts you upload. Make them feel like they are being spoken to and not spoken at. Take their needs and preferences into consideration, and you will win over your target audience with time. Califia Farms' content revolves around their target audience--from the locations they use for their photos, to their captions they write under their images and videos and even to the models they use in their photos. They put great thought into showing their followers and their target audience that they care. And their strategies have yielded great results. That is how important it is to know your target audience. It's one of the major determining factors for the success of your brand. Center your content around your target audience, and you won't go wrong. Create content that will make someone want to respond to it. Take time to plan your content; that's how you will be able to deduce whether it will be engaging and relevant to your target audience.

Tentsile Tree Tents (@tentsile)

Who Are They?

Tentsile Tree Tents is a company that manufactures tents for campers, backpackers and adventurers.

The London-based company caters to a problem many campers experience—rocky ground underneath their tents. To improve the campers' experience, Tentsile Tree Tents manufactured tents that can be set up above the ground. All that is needed are three sturdy trees to attach the ends of the tent. Once off the ground, up to three or four people can be accommodated by the structure. Their outdoor sleeping experience becomes a more comfortable one.

Now, this sounds like a product that has a very particular target audience—campers. The product gives little to work with when it comes to creating aesthetically pleasing images. One wouldn't think that a tent-making company would be interested in advertising on Instagram–an application solely dedicated to imagery. But Tentsile Tree Tents proved many wrong. With a great amount of creativity, the brand has managed to attain over 170,000 followers on Instagram, with the majority of the followership being engaged. That is quite a feat for a company that sells a product many advertisers would write off of marketing. That's quite a feat for any company, really.

But it is a feat the company managed to achieve, and now the company is one of the most sought-after companies when people are interested in purchasing camping gear. The Tentsile Instagram blog is known for its breathtaking images, whilst managing to strategically position their tents in the view. The brand has managed to attract an audience that goes beyond their target audience! People with and without a love for camping visit the blog regularly to view the stunning imagery found on the Instagram blog.

Tentsile has won further brownie points by being a brand that cares about the environment. For every tent bought, the company plants three trees. You can imagine how many trees the company has managed to plant since its growth!

Tentsile managed to take an idea that seemed to be 'too specific,' and they proved their critics and naysayers wrong. They created a global experience out of their idea. They went on to further take their marketing strategy to a global scale. One would have expected the blog to only attract followers who would be interested in the concept of camping. But they've managed to build their brand around people's love for travel and beautiful sights. They expanded their target audience by appealing to a desire many people have–the desire to travel and experience breathtaking scenery. They managed to cover two parts of the Travel niche–camping and sightseeing. It takes great skill, planning and thinking to be able to achieve such success. This a brand many can learn from. They've managed to take challenges that would often hinder the success of other brands, and they made it work in their favor. As they showcase different sights, with their tents positioned in the shots, they are managing to inspire campers and people who have never camped before to purchase their products and experience the sights they find on Tentsile's Instagram blog.

What Made Them Successful?

They thought out of the box. Tentsile went beyond just marketing their tents. They used their Instagram blog to market the camping experience. The tent always manages to blend in with their environment, but it still stands out as the product being marketed. When you go through Tentsile's Instagram blog, you will get a substantial feel of the camping experience. The locations featured on the Instagram blog are rainforests, mountaintops, hillsides, beaches and deserts. By depicting different locations, Tentsile is also showcasing the versatility of their product. It's genius, really.

The blog brings out the adventurer in the viewer. It appeals to the curiosity of many people. People have a desire to explore and visit hidden parts of the world. One of the things that keeps a lot of people from going camping is the thought of sleeping on the rough ground, uncomfortably. Tentsile took care of two issues. They have provided a glimpse into the places many wishes to see, and they have provided a comfortable way to go about it. They have improved the camping experience, and they have shown it to be the beautiful experience that it really is. Many people are put off by the idea of camping because they think of dirt, insects and discomfort. Tentsile has gone and proved them wrong and showed them how much of a lifetime experience camping is.

Not only are the pictures stunning, they are realistic as well. The locations exist, and they are actually even better in person.

The brand also made use of contests to encourage their followers to have the camping experience–on Tentsile's bill. This encourages more people to join in on the blog and engage with the brand. They have managed to cultivate hashtags that are particular to itself which has allowed them to increase their organic reach. The brand also organizes events and programs, such as traveling to certain destinations as groups. They don't just encourage people to go camping; they provide the opportunities as well. They make sure they let their followers know that they have got them covered.

Tentsile went all out with their campaign strategies. They acknowledged that their product would be hard to sell if they did not come up with larger-than-life ideas. Not only did they come up with such ideas they executed them *perfectly.* The Tentsile Instagram feed is a perfectly curated blog. All of the posts relate to each other and communicate the same message–they promote the product as well as the experience. The posts also evoke a reaction from their followers. This is because of how aesthetically pleasing they are. The pictures are so stunning, one can't help but exclaim, "Wow!" when they see them. Followers also message the brand to ask questions and receive more information on the tents, the locations showcased and the camping experience. This is increased engagement. Tentsile made sure they covered all areas when it came to coming up with strategies. They made sure they left their followers with as few questions to ask as possible. They paid attention to details and when a brand takes time to do something like that, there is no way their brand won't become successful.

They weren't afraid to take risks. Tentsile took a major risk. As mentioned at the beginning of this section, on paper, Tentsile is just about selling tents that can be set up above the ground. When you look at the idea that way, you don't think an Instagram blog would help the brand. "What will they post on Instagram besides pictures of tents?" someone might think. Well, they took it several levels higher. They did post pictures of tents. But no one expected them to showcase their product in such an innovative way.

In order to produce such high-quality images, money was definitely required. A lot of money was actually required to bring this brand to life. But it worked out for them. Sometimes you have to take risks in order to move forward. This is why you need to be confident in your brand. There are times you will have to convince people why your brand is so outstanding. Tentsile is 100% sold on their brand. The amount of effort they poured into it is clear evidence of this. They took a risk, and it paid off.

They managed to carve paths in two niches at the same time. They took the concept of wanderlust and used to it to reel in followers. The brand is also known to have strong customer service. They engage with their followers and ensure that all their needs are met. Follower morale is a priority with Tentsile and it has worked out well. By putting their followers first, they have managed to become a leading brand in the travel niche.

Their hard work and their risk-taking proved to be worthwhile.

The way the brand has set itself up, it has also created many venues for partnership. Companies from different niches will be interested in partnering with the brand because of the diversity it represents. This poses as a financial benefit for the brand.

They took up a cause. Tentsile appealed to another audience–those who are concerned about the wellbeing of the environment. In Tentsile's bio on Instagram, they made it clear that a part of the proceeds they receive go to bettering the environment. In an age where the fate of the environment is shaky, Tentsile has chosen to be a part of making sure that we live in a green world. They also use their brand to promote this cause, and they encourage their followers to be a part of it. The brand has gone beyond trying to make a profit. Tentsile has made the brand much more about themselves.

This is an honorable approach, but it also works in the favor of the brand from a brand-building perspective. People love brands that show that they care about more than themselves. They are moved by charitable actions, and they feel compelled to be a part of it. Tentsile isn't just building a followership. They are building a community–which will play to their strengths very well. The followership they build will be a very solid one, and this will lead to an impact that goes beyond the brand itself. The environment benefits from Tentsile's cause and call to action.

This could actually be seen as an unintentional campaign strategy. The more the cause grows, the more traffic is driven to the Tentsile's blog. More people will be interested in what the brand has to offer. More people will be interested in investing in what the brand has to offer.

What Can You Learn from Them?

Be as creative as you can possibly be. If there is something you can learn from Tentsile, learn that almost any kind of brand can be built on Instagram–as long as the person or people behind it are willing to go all-out to make sure that they can do it. If you are willing to go the extra mile, and beyond, in order to cultivate a brand that expresses originality and manages to maintain your followers' attention, go for it. Let your confidence carry you in this process; it will open your eyes to potential avenues that are worth investigating. A great idea isn't built in a day.

This does not mean attempt to use random strategies and hope one works out. No, that is not what Tentsile did. This is why planning continues to be emphasized. It's in these planning sessions you will be able to find the ideas and strategies that could fit best in building your brand–which is the ultimate goal. Don't throw any ideas out. If it looks like it has the potential to contribute to your brand, keep it, and test it out if you can. If it does not bring about the desired results, leave it. If the potential of the strategy increases, find ways to make the most of it.

These are a few of the many strategies one can use to grow their brand on Instagram. In the next chapter, we will speak on more strategies to assist you with increasing your reach on Instagram and growing your following.

Mistakes Brands Make That Lead to Their Failure on Instagram

You would be surprised to find that there are a number of major brands that are failing to build their brand on Instagram.

They Are Overly Promotional

A number of mega brands end up filling their blogs with content that lacks personality, lacks relatability and is solely for the sake of promoting the brand. The posts don't seek to engage with the followers. The captions Eventually, followers become interested in what the brands are posting and they withdraw from them.

They Do Not Pay Attention to the Quality of Their Images

Some brands upload pixelated posts with generic captions. The posts do not relate to one another, and when first-time viewers come to the blog, they are disappointed with what they see. Their expectations are not met, and they simply close the blog and are likely to not return to it again.

They Do Not Post Frequently

Posts are uploaded sporadically. The brand's inconsistency gives the impression that they aren't interested in the platform or in giving their followers something to see. With the way Instagram's algorithm is set up, it would be very hard for their posts to appear in their followers' feeds.

They Do Not Capitalize on Their Popularity

One would expect popular brands to use their popularity to build their brand on Instagram. It's a benefit they should take advantage of. But some of them don't. They are lax in their approach, and this shortchanges their reach on Instagram.

They Do Not Have a Goal-Driven Strategy

When you look at how some brands use their Instagram blogs, you can see that very little thought was put into their execution. The posts don't correlate in any way. These brands post sporadically, and one ends up being unsure of what they are trying to achieve.

They Buy Followers/Engagements

This practice is more common than expected amongst many brands and individuals on Instagram. But it is also a very crass way to operate on Instagram. It is very easy to tell when a blog has bought followers. The likes remain low. The engagement remain low. Eventually, the brands lose credibility on the platform, and their blog is considered dormant or ineffective.

Growth Strategies: How to Gain More Followers

This chapter will take you through strategies that will help you grow your followers in a legitimate way. Follower growth and engagement are the most important part of an Instagram blog's success; you cannot thrive without them. In this chapter, we will go into detail on the methods that will help you best when it comes to attracting new followers and maintaining your 'old' followers.

Consider these questions first before reading further:

Strategy 1. Make Your Blog Consistent

Consistency is an important part of becoming successful. It is also a major part of growing a large following on social media.

Consistency in Posting

When it comes to maintaining your blog, you have to be consistent with your uploading.

You can use a number of strategies to grow your followers, but if you are not feeding them interesting content regularly, you will have little to no engagement with your followers. They will end up becoming ghost followers, and all of your efforts will have been for nothing. This may sound a little dramatic, but this is true.

There are a number of individuals who made the mistake of resorting to means like buying followers and similar efforts to grow their following. Many of them assumed that when other people see their large following, they will follow the blog. This is a hit-or-miss approach that usually results in far more misses than hits. If you are considering taking this kind of route, don't. It's not worth it.

Building your following through genuine means is rewarding for you and your brand or business. You will be able to market your services or showcase your skills or products to followers who are genuinely interested in who you are and what you are about.

In order for them to know this you need to give them that information on a constant basis. You need to post regularly. If you intend on having a blog that is above average, you need to post above the average rate. This does not mean you need to upload twenty posts at the same time. You will end up driving your followers away. A balance needs to be found.

"Is this really important?" you may ask. Yes, it is. *Very* important.

In 2015, Quintly, a social media analytics tool, conducted a study that deduced that the average Instagram user posts at least once a day. Quintly also deduced that Instagram blogs with large followings posted with a higher frequency. Blogs with a high number of fans were seen to post at least two or three photos a day–on average.

A little over a year ago, Instagram rolled out a new, algorithm-based timeline–far different than its former chronological timeline. While the algorithm may not be easy to decipher, it is apparent that posting consistency is a key element to getting followers to view your posts regularly. Posts that are uploaded on a constant basis, and have a high level of engagement, are believed to be the types of posts that will be placed at the top of your followers' feeds.

Algorithm aside, consistent posting keeps you at the front of your followers' minds. If they are seeing your posts several times a day–and the content is interesting–the chances of increased follower engagement is higher.

Consistency in Appearance

Consistency, however, isn't just in posting. Your Instagram feed needs to be consistent in appearance as well. The aesthetics of your Instagram feed matters. If you are really serious about growing your following, you have to go the extra mile here as well.

Uploading a number of posts daily that do not relate to each other–or your niche--will not help you. The content you upload needs to be unifying at all times.

You need to ensure that your Instagram feed depicts consistency. First-time viewers should be able to deduce what your blog is about when they come across your blog.

Well-curated Instagram blogs are known to attract more followers. They are intriguing, and they inspire the viewer to peruse the feed more. Think about a number of blogs you find interesting. Take a look at their blogs–you will find that there is a form of uniformity on most of them. This is neither an accident or coincidence. It is a strategy.

Well-curated blogs give one the impression that the business or individual represented by the blog is organized and pays attention to detail. Well curated blogs are also aesthetically pleasing–which is what Instagram is all about. You could have the best services to offer in the world, but if your timeline is filled with random posts that are hard to understand–no matter how consistent they may be–the level of followers and engagements on your blog will remain low.

These are a couple of the best ways to achieve a well-curated blog:

Center Your Instagram Blog Around a Particular Theme

An easy way to curate your content is to center your blog around a particular theme. Themes can range from colors to culture, to book and movie concepts and even emotions–the list is endless. The content you upload should visually represent the theme you have centered your blog around–and your followers should be able to understand this. The themed content is for your followers and their attention; if they do not understand what your blog is based on, then your attempts have failed. If your followers don't understand your blog's theme, you will need to go back to the drawing board and revise your theme, your content, and make sure that you are creating content that is for your target audience–refer to the "Effective Communication" chapter for this.

For example, if your Instagram blog is for the sole purpose of displaying your work as a photographer, try and look for a particular set of colors to incorporate into your photography. You could decide to base your photography on warm colors (Warm color hues range from red to yellow) and create a fiery-colored theme (red, orange and yellow).

If you aren't able to base your blog on one theme, you could look to doing monthly themes. Every month your posts could be based on a different topic (that still relates to what your blog is originally about). This could be a good approach, too, as it'll build curiosity and intrigue amongst your followers. It is also a good way to stand out amongst others who may be in your niche.

Here are a couple of examples of popular Instagram accounts that are based on a particular theme:

Kat Gaskin (@katgaskin)

Kat Gaskin is a trailblazing entrepreneur and content creator who is making waves (pun intended) with the creative—and tropical—content she makes; she is also a travel blogger who spends a lot of her time traveling the world and capturing beaches on her blog and on her Instagram. It's no surprise that she based her Instagram blog on a specific tropical theme, making use of the stunning beach-themed photos she captures and a predominantly pastel color pallete (colors between soft blues and soft pinks).

One of her signature trademarks is including pineapples in her photos—just for the sake of doing so. Pineapples fit in with her tropical theme, and they add to the vibrance exuded by her Instagram blog; pineapples are also affiliated with one of her ventures—Salty Pineapple—a company that deals with generating design solutions for clients. The moment first-time viewers come across her page, they are immediately drawn in by the tropical theme, and they can immediately deduce what the blog is all about. Every photo Kat Gaskin uploads has to do with what her brand entails—freedom, bright colors and beautiful beaches. As you can see from the screenshots, every upload is related to the photo that was uploaded before it and the photo that was uploaded afterward—there is consistency. The theme expresses her personality, too—which is what her brand is based on; Kat left her regular nine-to-five job to pursue a career she built for herself, and it's working out for her. A well-themed blog like this also catches the attention of other companies and brands that are interested in having Kat as a representative for their products and services--good work always sells.

This Instagram account is good for both **lifestyle** and **travel** bloggers to take a look at when thinking of how to curate their Instagram blogs.

Oh.SoPretty (@oh.sopretty)

This example is the total opposite of the first one.

Oh.SoPretty is an excellent example of how one can use a simple theme to stand out on the platform. The blog does not make use of a lot of colors, as seen in the below screenshots. Instead, the lifestyle blogger opted for a black and white with a pop of color theme to give her blog a modern and artistic feel to it–and it worked. Every single post has the same color theme incorporated into it, and when you take a look at the photos, you can tell that it took a lot of planning, a creative eye and a lot of work to create such a harmonious Instagram page.

Minimalism is becoming a popular preference for many Instagram bloggers–regardless of their niche. Minimalist posts have a way of letting the audience focus on the content without being distracted by unnecessary colors and/or elements that did not belong in the image in the first place. The minimalist approach that Oh.SoPretty follows also gives the audience an impression that the blogger is an organized individual who always pays attention to detail–Instagram users are drawn to accounts where the creators have paid great attention to detail. You can also find elements of what was discussed in the "Effective Content" chapter: high-quality images with well-structured components and a consistent theme that represents the blog and the brand. A minimalist theme like the one depicted in the above screenshots are good for blogs from any niche; themes like this are more about using the props and colors you have wisely. There are many ways one can be creative with this theme.

Alternatively, you can choose an aesthetic for your blog.

Basically, an Instagram aesthetic is the 'vibe' your blog is affiliated with. It is what people see and feel whenever they come across your blog on Instagram. Instagram aesthetics range from blog to blog, but it is up to you to decide what kind of aesthetic you would like your blog to have. By this point of the book, you should know your target audience and the kind of content you would like to post; this puts you in the right space to determine the aesthetic for your Instagram feed.

Bloggers tend to establish an aesthetic for their blogs instead of basing their blogs on one theme or a set of recurring themes because an Instagram aesthetic offers more freedom. Your posts don't have to revolve around a limiting theme. Instead, you can tailor your posts to create a general vibe for your page.

It's clear, from the above screenshots, that this brand has established an aesthetic that says, "natural, young, and active." The brand makes use of a bright color palette (bright greens, oranges, blues, yellows, reds and pinks), natural backgrounds and components, as well as young models, to establish their aesthetic. When people think of Califia Farms, this is what they will envision in their minds. This aesthetic is specific to the brand and has, thus, become its own—it has become part of the brand. This aesthetic was created through the uploading of photos and a couple of videos that relate to each other. The content may vary in appearance, but it all connects in one way or another; every post contributes to the brand's established aesthetic. When someone comes across the blog, they experience the emotions the blog is trying to evoke from its audience—happiness, hyperactivity and excitement. One look at this blog and all you want to do is immerse yourself in everything the brand is about; you become encouraged to purchase the beverages and experience what everyone in the pictures is experiencing.

Let's take a look at the other brand example we mentioned in the previous chapter, Tentsile. A lot was said about the brand and its out-of-the-box strategies, but here we are only going to focus on the blog's aesthetic.

You can tell that the brand has an aesthetic of its own that speaks what the brand is founded on, "nature, adventure and tents." The blog is pleasant to look, at and it makes you want to scroll down and see more. The collective images evoke a reaction from the brand's audience–the desire to travel and experience these places in real life. The blog's aesthetic has a common emotion–calmness–and evokes an emotion from the audience–relaxation. When you look at the blog, all you want to do is find a tent, like the one in the images, and lie down in the midst of a beautiful surrounding. If you look carefully, you will see that every photo is based in a different location across the globe, but this has not detracted from the blog's aesthetic in any way. The brand has managed to combine photos that would look random on their own in a way that makes them look united. They all relate in one way or another, and they communicate the central theme of the brand—traveling and tents.

The third example of a well-curated Instagram blog comes from a well-known food blog, @cookinwithmima. Mariam E. is the brains and hands behind the popular Instagram blog. When you take a look at her blog, you will understand why she is so successful.

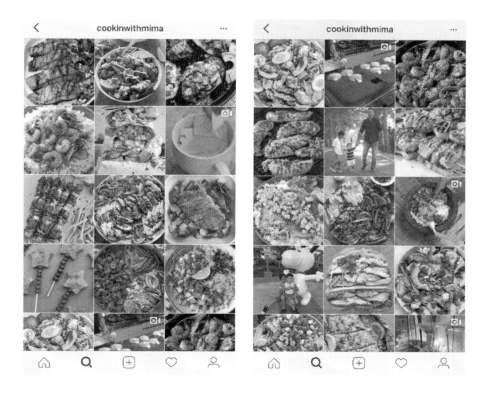

Mariam's blog exudes vibrancy with the brightly-colored food, the exotic ingredients she added to the foods and the creative plating styles that add to the overall aesthetic of the example of that. If your page is unable to stick to one color palette in particular, don't stress yourself. Channel your focus into making sure that every post that follows the other complements the next post in one way or another. Take a look at @cookinwithmima's page. You can see that the foods in every post are different, the colors are different and the style in which the foods are arranged are different, but when you look at the page as a whole, you notice that every post contributes to the blog's aesthetic. When you look at the blog, you see great food that makes you hungry. When you think of @cookingwithmima your mind immediately takes you to what you saw when you went through the page. That is when you know that a blog's aesthetic is successful—when the viewer is able to remember it long after they have viewed the blog.

The key to establishing your blog's aesthetic is to ensure that your posts flow with one another. You will not be able to maintain an aesthetic for your Instagram blog if your posts are random and unrelated. Consistency needs to be in your blog's appearance as a whole. You cannot afford to forget that your blog is in competition with hundreds of blogs in your niche; you cannot afford to slack when it comes to your blog's appearance. If you intend on having a well-curated blog, you need to put in the time required to plan your posts in advance. This is where scheduling posts come into play.

Scheduling Your Posts

Scheduling your posts can be beneficial for your blog and building your brand in the following areas:

Organization

Scheduling your posts allows you to stay organized when it comes to handling your Instagram blog. Planning in advance allows you to tailor your blog's appearance. With enough time, this will allow you to pay attention to detail and ensure that your blog maintains the aesthetic you initially established for your blog. You will also be able to ensure that your posts remain consistent with one another. Scheduling allows you to plan the days and times your posts are uploaded onto Instagram; this, in turn, will allow you to upload your posts consistently. It's advisable to set aside a couple of hours to plan at least 10 to 20 of the next posts you intende to upload on Instagram.

Planning your posts in advance also allows you to come up with the perfect captions and the perfect hashtags for the posts. The last thing you want to do is rush your captions and hashtags. Captions are a major part of engaging with your followers; if your captions are not effective, you will hinder your progress with your followers. When you plan your posts on a grid—which is what most scheduling applications will give you as a platform to plan your posts—you will be able to see the full appearance of your blog. You will be able to see which posts look best next to each other, and you will also be able to detect and resolve any unnecessary repetition or inconsistencies. When you work in advance, you are able to plan with a clear mind which will prevent any mistakes from occurring, too.

Strategy

Instagram does not have a feature on the application that will allow you to schedule posts. There are many online and mobile applications you can use to schedule your posts. Many of these applications offer you the option to observe the analytics for your blog. When you view the analytics for your blog, you will be able to determine the best times to upload your posts onto Instagram. 'Best times' are categorized by the times of the day where your posts will be viewed by most of your followers–which will lead to increased engagements. When you know the best times to upload your posts, this will allow you to schedule your posts effectively. This is one of the simplest ways to ensure that you will be able to attract the attention of your followers–by knowing when they are usually online. This will lead to your blog having a series of posts being uploaded at the best time consistently, which will result in your blog pulling in follower engagements *consistently.* Instagram's algorithm is designed to promote Instagram blogs–and their posts–that have consistent follower engagements. Once your blog is being promoted regularly, because of the high number of engagements it receives, your following will grow–which is what one of your goals as an Instagram blogger should be. Scheduling your posts on Instagram according to the analytics provided by any app or tool you use–provided the analytics are accurate–will be a very strategic move on your part.

Convenience

Unfortunately, Instagram does not allow third-party posting, so you will not be able to auto-upload your posts–but this won't be much of an issue. Scheduling your posts helps you take care of the major work when it comes to uploading content onto your blog. All that will be left for you to do is post at the times you have scheduled; most applications come with a reminder feature that will ensure that you are aware of what time you need to post on the scheduled day. Some applications have an option that will allow you to upload from the scheduling app directly onto Instagram–with a couple of steps in between. This means that you will have more time to yourself on your hands once you have scheduled your posts, and all that will be left for you to do is post on the scheduled days. This free time will give you the opportunity to perform other tasks without interruption–tasks like researching marketing strategies, interacting with your followers and fellow Instagram bloggers, taking care of other business-related matters or even taking care of your own personal tasks. Scheduling posts allows you to have a more flexible timeline– which is something you will need when you have many tasks to deal with. In some instances, scheduling your posts also allows you to take breaks from social media–which is much needed at times. Sometimes we can get so caught up with trying to keep our blogs on top, we forget to tend to matters in our real lives. When you are able to plan your posts in advance, you are freeing up time during the course of the week to cater to you and your needs–which is important.

There are several mobile applications you can use to schedule posts and arrange the order in which you'd like the posts to appear.

Some of the apps you can try out are:

Planoly

Planoly is a favorite amongst Instagram users. The app comes with a wide variety of features.

The app offers a fifteen-day trial. When the trial expires, you'll have to subscribe and pay for it as a service. That is one of its downsides. If you are really set on doing all that's required to ensure your Instagram feed is as organized as possible–this app is good for you.

PLANN

PLANN is another firm favorite amongst Instagram users. The multi award-winning app comes with a team sharing feature–which is very useful for businesses and other teams. You will also be able to store your hashtags as groups–which makes the job of adding hashtags to your posts much easier. If you are a blogger, creative or business owner–this is the app for you. The app is free to install, but it does come with a few in-app purchases.

Mosaico

Mosaico is a user-friendly app. If you are looking for an app without the bells and whistles, but still does the job well, this is the app for you. The app will cost $5.99 (one off). This app, however, is not available on Android devices.

UNUM

UNUM is an app that was recommended by a number of social media users. It offers similar features to *Planoly* and *PLANN,* but it does have a couple of shortfalls. Some users have complained of struggling with arranging their photos on the grid. The app is free to install, but it also comes with a couple of in-app purchases.

Step-By-Step Process for Using a Scheduling Tool

In this example, we will use the Planoly application.

1. Download the application from your device's App Store.

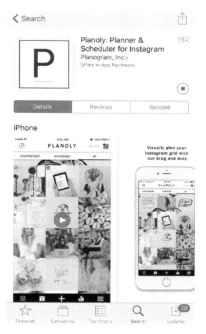

2. Open the application, and create an account. The application will ask for your Instagram account details in order for your account to be created.

3. Once your account has been created, and you've logged in, you will see three tabs titled: Unscheduled, Scheduled, and All.

   The Unscheduled tab is for the posts you have uploaded and arranged on the grid but haven't scheduled yet.

The Scheduled tab will show you the photos you have scheduled to be posted.

The All tab will show you both scheduled and unscheduled posts.

4. The grid in the above screenshot is an example of a planned grid. The grid resembles the grid you have on Instagram. You can swap photos around, add new ones or remove the ones you don't like.

5. To add a photo, tap the plus (+) symbol. It will take you to a list of folders where you can get a photo of your

choice. Select the photo (or photos) you would like to upload and select the 'add' option.

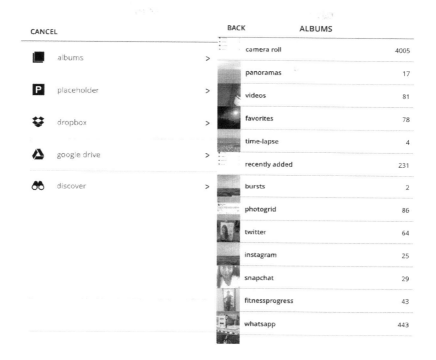

CANCEL		BACK	ALBUMS	
albums	>	camera roll		4005
placeholder	>	panoramas		17
		videos		81
dropbox	>	favorites		78
google drive	>	time-lapse		4
		recently added		231
discover	>	bursts		2
		photogrid		86
		twitter		64
		instagram		25
		snapchat		29
		fitnessprogress		43
		whatsapp		443

6. Once you've added your photos, you can arrange them on the grid until you are happy with what you see. To arrange your photos, just hold them down with a finger, and move them around the screen.

71

CANCEL   DELETE

 Sent via @planoly #planoly

schedule

scheduled at

or Post Now

UPDATE

7. Once you've arranged your photos, you can begin to schedule them. Select a photo that hasn't been scheduled; you'll be taken to a screen that will allow you to add a caption and hashtags to your photo. Below the image, there is a 'schedule' option. Turn it on.

8. Use the 'schedule at' option to set the day and time for your photo, and update your settings by tapping the 'update' option at the bottom of the screen. *Voila!* You

have successfully scheduled a photo. Repeat the process with the other ones until you are done.

Strategy 2. How to Grow Using Hashtags

This is a strategy that you cannot afford to overlook. Hashtags are part of the lifeblood of Instagram. If you have any intention of growing your followers on Instagram, you will need to incorporate hashtags into your posts. The reason you need to use hashtags is to increase your organic reach. Organic reach is the number of unique people who are shown your post– without the use of paid distribution.

Hashtags serve as keywords, or indexes, for your blog and your blog posts; when users on Instagram search particular words, if these words were used as hashtags for your blog post(s), there is a higher chance of your posts appearing in users' search results. If your tagging is done correctly, your posts could be in the top tier of Instagram users' search results.

Your use of hashtags, however, needs to be done with great thinking and resourcefulness. Using hashtags like *#green, #food, #happy* won't get you very far. You need to find hashtags that are relevant to your posts and are also able to connect with a large amount of Instagram users.

Using hashtags is also a form of marketing your brand on Instagram–which is extremely necessary. Your competitors will also be vying for the top tier in users' search results when they search for keywords that relate to your particular niche. If you choose to neglect the use of hashtags, you might as well give up on any hope of standing out among your competitors.

You need to use every single feature Instagram offers you, and you need to use them well.

Hashtags also contribute to your chances of having your blog trend on Instagram. When you constantly share high-quality photos that are related to your brand, the chances of users picking up your photos and sharing them across the platform increases. When this happens, your Instagram blog will start to trend, which will pull in more followers for your blog–people are more likely to become invested in trending blogs because they have seen proof that you have something that will be of interest to them.

This is a Step-by-Step Process to Identify Quality Hashtags for Your Blog:

1. **Identify the common hashtags being used by influencers in your niche.**

   Influencers are users on Instagram who have a high following and are able to sway the opinions of their followers. It would be good for you to review their posts and find the common hashtags they use under their posts. Pick out the ones that are relevant to your posts and store them.

2. **Find related hashtags to the ones you picked out.**

   You can use a site like *Hashtagify.me* to do this. It is a popular, straightforward site that will help you locate more popular hashtags that will be relevant to your posts. Only pick the hashtags that are related to your niche. Do not just copy and paste. This will dilute the efficacy of what you are trying to do.

3. Measure the relevance of the hashtags.

There are a number of sites and engines you can use to gauge the relevance of your hashtags. Some of the recommended ones are *RiteTag, Hashtag.org,* and *PromoRepublic.* They are all accessible on the Internet, and they offer similar services.

You can also base your hashtags on your brand. Ideally, you should desire that your brand, and not some random result, pop up in users' search results when they search for your brand name or if they use keywords that relate to your brand. The solution to this is to include hashtags with your brand name under as many of your posts as possible. This will create an index filled with your posts that will be displayed in users' search results whenever they search anything related to your brand. In order for this to work, though, you need to post these hashtags *consistently.* It won't happen in a few days, and it might not happen in a couple of months, but you will still need to remain consistent. As your blog grows in popularity on Instagram, more and more users will search for your brand and they will be directed to your Instagram blog–if they are convinced by what they see on your blog, they will end up following your Instagram blog.

Once you have found a group of hashtags that are relevant to your niche, and relevant on Instagram, examine all of them, and try to cut them down to a maximum of 35. Instagram has a limit of 30 hashtags per post, so you can interchange a few of them when uploading different posts.

A Few Examples of Top Hashtag Campaigns:

1. Adidas Originals

The sportswear giant made use of the hashtag #ORIGINALis, and collaborated with a number of top celebrities to promote their latest line of fashion. This campaign was mainly targeted at lovers of the hip hop culture and community—and the sale of products was a great success thanks to the campaign.

2. Airbnb

The innovative accommodation giant used Instagram to promote tolerance and acceptance across all genders, religions, sexual preferences, races and nationalities by using the hashtag #WeAccept. The campaign was a timely one as the brand established its stance on a topic that was the rage at the time, and it managed to solidify the brand's consumer base.

3. Amazon

Sales giant, Amazon, made use of Instagram to run a campaign that expressed their gratitude to their users and supporters for getting them to number one in their corporate standing. The company used the hashtag #1 to carry their campaign; needless to say, it was a hit.

4. Nintendo

Gaming masters, Nintendo, resorted to using Instagram to build a buzz for their launch of their latest product–the Nintendo Switch. They made use of the hashtags #NintendoSwitch and #12Switch to get their followers to join in on the hype–and it worked in their favor.

Strategy 3. Sharing User Generated Content

Sharing user generated content is one of the best things you can do for your brand–especially if your brand involves retail. User generated content is simply content that is created by your customers and/or your followers; it comes in the form of photos taken by users, product or service reviews or photo contests. Sharing user generated content is a good way to gain the attention of many other followers. People want to know that their opinions matter, and this is what sharing user generated content is all about–showing your followers that you pay attention to their profiles and their voices just as much as they pay attention to your brand. Mega brands take this need people have, and they capitalize it through sharing the content their customers and followers share on their personal profiles.

Sharing user generated content is simple really–find content pertaining to your brand, generated by your followers and share it on your Instagram feed–don't forget to credit the user by tagging their handle in the caption. If you do this on a continuous basis, you will generate a buzz around your brand. Once users become aware that your brand is sharing their content on your Instagram blog, they will become inspired to generate more content in hopes of catching your attention and having their content shared.

Adding user generated content to your Instagram blog is also a creative and dynamic way of sourcing diverse content for your blog; it also contributes to building your brand and further establishing your brand on Instagram.

Sharing user generated content is important for brands because it contributes to building an engaged community through sharing content that the audience will love and appreciate. Instagram is one of the best platforms for brands to genuinely connect with their audience in an almost one-on-one kind of way. Making use of the user generated content is a brand's way of allowing real people–members of their audience–the chance to tell their own stories on the brand's platform; the brand is giving their followers exposure by showcasing their content to the brand's following. There is a certain kind of authenticity that comes from sharing user generated content that is hard to find in content generated by brands. It is that very authenticity that allows followers to connect with a brand better in comparison to its competitors. This a strategy that will work the best with the current millennial generation because this is what millennials live for–experiences. Brands have realized that it will take more than sharing promotional content to win over a millennial audience–the audience that holds the spending power; brands have to incorporate experiences and emotions into their content in order to genuinely connect with the millennial audience. According to research from a number of marketing companies, millennials and parts of other generations are more likely to trust user generated content in comparison to content generated by brands and the media. The reason why people are so sold on user generated content is because when the creator created the content, they created it with no ulterior motive; they simply wanted to add to the digital conversation.

If your brand is based in retail–selling of products–or in the offering of services, it will be easier for you to start sharing user generated content. When interacting with your customers and clients, encourage them to share their thoughts on your brand on their Instagram accounts. When they tag you in their posts, share their post on your blog and credit them. This serves as a means of promotion for your brand by sharing positive reviews from your customers and clients, and it also creates conversation among your followers–your followers will be inspired to comment on the user generated post you uploaded because they will feel that they can relate more with the user's opinions. The more user generated content you share, the more it will generate engagement among your community of followers. You need to be careful not to end up diluting your brand's organic content with user generated content–find a way to strike a balance.

User generated content also allows your brand to keep up to date with your followers and how they feel about your brand and the content you are providing your followers. Sharing user generated content will force you to be aware of the types of followers you have; knowing your followers helps you confirm whether you are really reaching out to your target market or if you need to reconsider who your target market actually is–this is a common thing. Sometimes, as you grow with your blogging and you get the hang of handling your brand, you may realize that your target audience may differ to what you initially thought your target audience. If you are running a beauty blog for young, working women, you may be surprised to find older women following your blog for advice; or if you are running a sports blog for athletes, you will find that people who aren't athletes are interested in what you have to offer.

Studies show that user generated content has the power to influence followers to take certain actions. Followers may feel inspired to buy the products they see in user's product reviews because they feel they can trust a 'real person's' opinion more than they can trust what the brand says about their own product. Social media users spend time on social media actively seeking user generated content that speaks about certain brands in order to determine whether they can align themselves with the brands or if they should look at different brands for the products or services they desire—most users go with what other users say. Brands have discovered this, and this is why they are trying to tap into the user generated content strategy in order to have access to the audiences with the greater influence and spending power.

You can also inspire your followers to generate content pertaining to your brand by creating hashtags that include your brand name, and ask your followers to create content and include the hashtag in their captions. This kills two birds with one stone—you are increasing the amount of user generated content you can access, and you are also creating a trend out of your brand through the hashtag you created for users to make use of.

User generated content is also a very exciting strategy because there are so many interesting and creative ways you can go about it. The key thing is determining the social angle you want to take; determine what you want the content to reflect on your brand. This is for the sake of finding direction in your approach because this can change with time—there is no problem with that. You also need to be confident in what your brand has to offer. If the content you are looking for are reviews on your brand, you need to make sure that the majority of the reviews are *genuinely* positive. If you try to doctor the content your users share, you are defeating the whole purpose of the user generated content. Remember that you serve as the guide in this strategy–you guide your users in the kind of content they should generate.

Here is an example of a brand that successfully executed a user generated campaign:

Starbucks

In April 2014, the mega brand launched the Starbucks' White Cup Contest. The contest encouraged customers from the U.S and Canada to participate in the challenge by decorating a Starbucks cup, taking a photo of the cup and submitting it via uploading on social media using the hashtag--#WhiteCupContest. The winning design would be featured in a limited edition of Starbucks' reusable plastic cups. In the space of three weeks, just under 4000 customers participated in the challenge and submitted their designs. The contest was a win for both Starbucks and the customers.

Starbucks received an overwhelming amount of publicity which helped solidify the brand's presence on social media. The challenge trended on all platforms of social media, and the account received a large number of followers in response to the challenge and the buzz it generated. The effects of this challenge remained with the brand as Starbucks soon became known as one of the brands that genuinely cares about customer feedback and morale.

The campaign benefited customers since the challenge served as a platform for users to showcase their artistic skills;

the campaign also gave customers and spectators the impression that the brand was interested in what the people had to say about the brand. Brands know that consumers are big on knowing that their concerns and opinions are heard–repeat this to yourself until it sticks in your head. The overwhelming response to the challenge also boosted Starbucks' reputation in the eyes of their customers and followers–people always respond to trending topics.

Running contests and challenges for your customers is a very good way to gain user generated content for your blog. You need to find ways to make them exciting so that people are encouraged to join in on the fun.

This strategy is very simple; it mainly requires you to understand your audience and communicate with them in a way that will get them on board with generating content your brand can share on your blog.

A Step-by-Step Walkthrough of How You Can Organize a Campaign Similar to Starbucks' Campaign.

1. Find a task the majority of your customers/followers will be able to do. (Starbucks' task was simple–draw designs on a cup).

2. Decide on a prize before launching the campaign–and make it worthwhile for your followers (Starbucks' prize was giving the winner an opportunity to have their cup's design feature in a limited Starbucks edition of plastic, reusable cups)

3. Think of a catchy hashtag your followers will be able to attach to their photos. (It can be as simple as Starbucks' hashtag - #WhiteCupContest)

4. Start advertising the campaign on your Instagram account–and any other social media platforms you may be a part of. You need to reel in as many participants as possible.

5. Make sure you let your followers know that they have to submit photos of their completed task via uploading the photo on their Instagram accounts and attaching the challenge/contest's hashtag.

6. Search the hashtag daily and make sure to repost the photos on your account–don't forget to tag the user, too.

7. Run the challenge for a scheduled duration of time–a month, for example–before announcing the winner.

It's as simple as that.

Strategy 4. Build Effective Collaborations

Collaborations can be an effective way for brands and bloggers to work together in order to promote themselves on Instagram. Commercial brands and corporations often take to collaborating with social media influencers in order to grow the reach for their brands. These companies know that social media influencers have direct access to their target market, and they know that these influencers have the power to convince their followers to make certain spending decisions. Many people are influenced by what they see on social media, and commercial brands and companies are capitalizing on this in order to increase their profit and establish their brands further. If your blog on Instagram has a large following and a high rate of engagement, you will have no problem with finding bigger brands and more popular Instagram users to work with. Your follower count and the rate of engagement on your blog are very important when it comes to collaborating with other Instagram users and commercial brands. They need to see that you have something they can benefit from, something that will improve their brands in a significant way. What they are looking for are new ways to tap into their target market. If you have what they want, then they will work with you.

If you are new to Instagram, or your brand is yet to become established on the platform, you might struggle with finding big brands and companies who will be ready to collaborate with you; they would prefer to work with more experienced and more established bloggers because they feel that they will be able to bring in more customers or more publicity for their brands. This does not mean that all hope is lost for you, though; it just means that you will need to start on a smaller scale instead.

This is how you can go about it:

Find accounts on Instagram that are in your niche or a niche that is similar to yours.

The best way to start collaborating, as a small-scale blogger and brand, is to find another small-scale blogger who has a similar or slightly larger following and the same amount of–or more--engagement as your blog. The idea here is to collaborate with each other as partners and help with building both brands; it is a mutually beneficial relationship. It would be advisable for you to find at least three or four users you would be interested in collaborating with so that you have options, and you won't be left stranded if any of them refuse to collaborate with you.

You can find these users through searching for hashtags from your niche and taking a look at the accounts that use them too–like we mentioned before, hashtags are one of the best ways to build a community on Instagram.

You could also use the 'Instagram Explore' option to find bloggers who are similar to your account. Instagram Explore displays posts from popular Instagram accounts and accounts you might be interested in following. If you want to see if they are interested in collaborating with you, follow them and engage with their content first. Instagram users are more likely to pay attention to what someone has to say if they notice that the user has been engaging with their content.

If they agree to collaborate with you, **build a rapport with them**. Don't just view this partnership as a way for your brand to benefit; take time to get to know the blogger as well. Personal bonds work better than strictly professional partnerships on social media–when followers notice a budding friendship between bloggers, they will be encouraged to be a part of it. Collaborations are one of the main ways influencers and celebrities build their brands, by combining fan bases through collaboration. Think of it this way. When you are collaborating with a fellow blogger, you can promote each other in the following ways:

- Share each other's posts on your respective blogs

- Create challenges for your followers, and treat it like a friendly competition

- Meet up in person, if possible, and create content together

- Promote the content you create together. You could create a hashtag that features both your brand names and encourage your followers to use it.

- As time goes by, if you are consistent with the collaborations, you will find that you and your co-collaborator will have managed to grow your followers and gain more popularity.

- Don't stop working together when you've reached your goals; use your partnership as a marketing strategy, too. Capitalize on the joint following you managed to amass.

The Main Objective is Engagement.

With all these strategies, the main thing you must remember is that you are trying to increase your engaged following. When you remember this, it will prevent you from trying to resort to dishonest ways of accumulating followers.

Ways You Should Not Consider Resorting to:

- **Random Following/Unfollowing**

  This is a strategy a number of up-and-coming blogs and aspiring influencers on Instagram resort to–following a large number of users on Instagram, waiting for them to follow back, and then unfollowing them in order to increase your follower-to-following ratio (the number of people following you versus the number of people you follow). People assume that if your follower count is higher than the number of people you are following, it means that your account is worth checking out and–ideally–following. This strategy, however, is rarely ever successful. When you follow random users on Instagram, you are not doing yourself a favor. You are deliberately ignoring reaching out to your target audience in order to access a few quick follows. In the rare cases that this works out for your blog, this strategy still won't benefit your blog because your rate of engagements will still be low. The people following you back won't be interested in what your blog has to offer, so whenever you upload content, they will simply scroll past your post on their feed without engaging with it. Your goal as an Instagram blogger shouldn't just be to have a large following; you should also aim to have a following that is engaged with your blog and the content you upload–that is how your brand will be built. Your brand will not be built on random, disengaged followers who will not be interested in what you have to offer.

Instagram users aren't ignorant either; they have become aware of accounts that randomly follow users for the sole purpose of unfollowing these users later in order to increase their follower-to-following ratio. Some users have resorted to unfollowing, or even blocking, Instagram accounts that take part in this strategy; the last thing you want to do is be known for being 'shady' or 'annoying' on Instagram–word travels. Stick to creating content for your target audience, and if you choose to follow users on Instagram, let it be users who are in your niche, and do not follow them with the intention of unfollowing them. If you gain a reputation for following and unfollowing users on Instagram, users won't take your brand seriously, and this will only hurt your brand in the long run.

- **Buying Followers or Likes.**

There are a number of third party applications that offer brands the opportunity to buy followers in order to increase their follower count. Instagram users who may be struggling to establish their brand on the platform often get drawn in by the thought of being able to easily access a large following for their accounts; they can purchase 100s, 1000s or 10,000s of followers and likes in order to 'boost' their blog; there is a popular belief that if your account has a large number of followers, then people will take your blog seriously. Resorting to buying followers or likes for your posts on Instagram is one of the most unwise decisions a blogger could make. Buying followers may increase your follower count, and it may give others the impression that your account is popular on Instagram, but you are actually shortchanging yourself because the followers you will be purchasing are ghost followers–followers who will not engage with your blog in anyway. There is nothing to boast of if you have a large following, but your posts are struggling to get up to 50 likes. The moment people notice this about your account, they will realize that your following isn't genuine. There are apps that have been created to detect Instagram accounts with fake followers; the last thing you want is for your account to be one of them. Applications that offer you the option to buy followers often have an ulterior motive–to use your account to post spam content. Once you purchase followers and make use of the application's services, you have given them a gateway to use your account to post content that is totally unrelated to your brand. Your brand will lose credibility on Instagram once people discover that you have bought followers; people will receive the impression that you are willing to use any shortcuts to get 'fame,' and that will rob you of your audience. Don't waste your money buying followers; put more effort into engaging with the genuine followers that you do have. It's better to have an account with 100s of followers who are very engaged with your brand, in comparison to having an account with 1000s of followers and little to no engagement.

- **Paying for Features/Shoutouts.**

Another mistake an Instagram blogger could make is resorting to paying popular accounts on Instagram to feature his or her post on the popular account's Instagram feed. At first glance, it may appear to be a sweet deal–you are paying for genuine engagement with the account's large following, but deals like this do not work in the long-term. Your post will just be one of many other posts the popular account will share on its blog; the most that will come from paying for a feature or a shoutout is a large number of likes–on the popular account's post, not yours–and a few new followers in your direction. Receiving a positive response from the account's followers isn't a guarantee, though–even if you are both in the same niche. Your individual post might not be enough to pull the attention of another account's followers. You also have to think of it like this: if this account is open to receiving payment to feature anyone's posts on their blog, it means that their content is not harmonious in nature. This means that there is a high chance that the account's audience might not be your target audience–even if you both belong to the same niche. Alternatively, the account might prioritize their content over anything they are paid to share, meaning that even if they share the post you pay them to share, they won't promote it in a way that will convince their followers to rush over to your blog. Followers can also detect when a feature is not sincere; this is why it's better to stick to collaborations where genuine relationships are built and the support you give each other is mutual.

Instagram users who have resorted to paying for features and/or shoutouts later went on to say they regretted their decision; some of them wish they had spent the money on something more beneficial. There are only so many features you can pay for; this option will not benefit your brand in the long term. Instead of spending money on features or shoutouts that won't help your brand in the long run, spend extra time engaging with your followers or researching better hashtags for your captions–these are activities that *will* help your brand in the long run. There really are no legitimate shortcuts to gaining a large, engaged following--it is hard work and you cannot cheat the process.

If you are able to maintain a blog that has a consistent aesthetic through uploading regularly and making use of quality hashtags, after some time you will witness the growth in your following on Instagram.

This is not a quick-fix strategy, however. It will take time, and it will require effort on your part. But this effort is worth it in the long run. When you find that your engagement with followers is increasing, you will be grateful for the effort you put in.

As mentioned at the beginning of this text, this is one of the basic strategies, but it is one many swear by. It will create substantial progress, and you won't have to consider paid means of distributing your posts for a while.

Stick to these strategies, and you will not be sorry.

Monetization: How to Start Making Money

Once you've managed to grow your following to a certain extent, the next thing you should look at is finding ways to monetize your Instagram account. That should be one of the main goals for your brand–to make money from what you do. There are diverse ways to generate income through your Instagram account, and we have listed a few below:

1. **Selling the caption space underneath your photo.**

   This is a minor way to make money on your Instagram account; it's a good way if you're looking for some money on the side whilst managing your brand. This option is also one of the least invasive methods for your account–you won't have to fill your Instagram feed with unrelated content for the sake of advertising. This option is often available to Instagram blogs with large followings. When posting your content, instead of adding your own caption, you can add a shoutout to another account that has paid for the caption space. You need to be careful with this option, however. Your caption space is still important for your own content. You can't afford to give it up all the time.

2. **Make use of the link in your bio.**

   Instagram gives users one space to upload a link on their bio for followers and first-time viewers to click on and be redirected to another link. If you post a link in your captions, they will not work. It's a downer for many users, but the platform hasn't budged on changing this—maybe in the future. This does not mean you cannot use the link space as a way to earn money through your Instagram account.

Many bloggers who are in the retail niche set up online stores or landing pages for product launches for their online clientele. They make use of the link space in their bio to encourage followers to click the link and be redirected to the online shop or the landing page. Another way to redirect followers' attention is to add "Click the link in my bio" in the captions underneath the posts they upload. Followers are reminded of the link and take time to check out what the bloggers have to offer. If your advertising is done right, your followers will be compelled to click the link on a frequent basis and purchase more of your products.

3. Become a brand representative.

This is a better option for bloggers who are running their accounts from a personal capacity e.g. lifestyle bloggers, food bloggers, travel bloggers, etc. If you run your account individually, it will be easier for your brand to serve as a platform for other brands to receive representation through you. You can think of being a brand representative as being part of a paid collaboration; instead of collaborating with a brand for publicity, you are also earning income for promoting their products or services.

Big, commercial brands are interested in working with Instagram accounts that have large followings, and a great rate of engagement with their followers, because this means that these accounts are able to influence their audience in a way that will benefit these commercial brands. For example, if your followers see you promoting content for a popular sportswear brand, they will be encouraged to buy products from that same brand because you support it–it's as simple as that.

Brands will often ask you to include their brand's name in your account's logo, and you may be required to cover their events and review their products on your Instagram account. They will pay you for your work, in return. Becoming brand representatives has helped a number of social media influencers gain a footing in the advertising industry--the same thing could happen for you if you are smart about it. You just need to make sure that your brand has something these companies are interested in.

The one thing you need to look out for, though, if you become a brand's representative, is that their products do not change the nature of your content. Mega brands can become domineering toward social media influencers once these influencers agree to promote their brands; some of them will try to get you to change your content completely and only post content that relates to the brand. This will not benefit you in any way because your blog will go from being the popular brand that followers are loyal to, to an Instagram account promoting products for mega brands and nothing else. Your followers will end up losing interest in your account, and you will lose out in the long run.

Remember to remain true to your brand; your brand is what got you the recognition in the first place.

4. Product placement

Product placement is a very popular way for Instagram users with popular accounts to make money without having to dilute their blog's content. The reason why some bloggers would prefer to earn money through product placement instead of becoming brand representatives is because they have more freedom and control when they aren't working for a brand directly. Many influencers have had bad experiences with mega brands that became imposing the moment influencers agreed to represent their brands, so they opted for the subtle alternative that is product placement instead. Product placement can be simply defined as including a brand or retailer's products in your photos–and occasionally giving them a shoutout when you upload them. A popular example of product placement is the 'Flat Tummy Te' movement.' If you take a look at a number of celebrity's pages–the Kardashians and Jenners are a good example–you will notice that they occasionally have posts where they are smiling and holding a carton of Flat Tummy Tea–tea designed to help consumers lose weight. If you look at the post captions, you will see a promotional review on the product. Something that will go along the lines of,

"I'm so grateful for this Flat Tummy Tea product. It helped me get rid of these stubborn pounds around my midsection, and I feel a lot healthier, too!"

At first glance, the posts will look like they were created as sincere forms of advice, but this isn't the case. These companies and brands pay individuals with large followings on their Instagram accounts to promote their products. The more influence an account has, the more money these accounts can charge interested brands and companies for 'space' on their blogs.

This is a suitable option for bloggers who are the faces of their brands and blogs—it will make it easier for them to make reviews and upload product-placed content without interfering with their brand's image.

5. **If your blog isn't into retail, consider creating products you can sell through your account.**

The route a number of Instagram bloggers take, once they have built a substantial following and they have firmly established their brand on the platform, is going into retail independently.

Instagram bloggers turn to creating their own clothing and product lines, and they use their followers as their target consumers. If they have managed to build a following that is loyal to their brand, their products will sell, and they will be well on their way to becoming successful entrepreneurs through social media.

The best way to go into this form of earning income is to start small. Since you know what your brand represents, and you are aware of your target audience and their preferences, you will know what to start with. Some users start with a T-shirt line; they print T-shirts with designs inspired by their brand, and they start to advertise them on their account. Their followers become interested in the product, and soon the blogger starts to generate sales through their platform. Once they have made a significant number of sales, they may move into a new product. For example, if they started with T-shirts, they can branch into product caps, hoodies, jackets and so on. This needs to be done with caution; however, you should only go into this line of monetization if you are confident that your followers will be interested in purchasing your products. If you go into this uncertain, you risk making a huge loss.

One of the major benefits of advertising your own product is that you will be able to remain true to what your brand represents without any interferences. Instead of bowing to the preferences of an external brand, you will be able to tailor your advertising campaigns around your original content; this will allow you to fully cater to your followers needs and earn good income at the same time.

These are just a few of the many ways one can use to monetize their Instagram accounts and earn good income. If you are able to use your business sense and advertising expertise—which you can easily learn through researching on the Internet—you will be able to create an even bigger business out of your brand. Don't be afraid to take risks with finding endorsements and diving into retail; risks are necessary if you intend on setting yourself apart from your competitors.

Lastly, don't be afraid to charge high prices if you know that your blog or brand is worth it. Some interested brands and companies may try to get you to lower your prices and exploit your work, but you need to be firm. If they walk away from the deal, it's not the end of the world. You will find brands, companies, and individuals who will be interested in your services—and they will accept your charges without forcing you to compromise.

Metrics: How to Track Your Progress

These are a number of paid (and free) platforms you can use to gauge your account's metrics if you want to see the effectiveness of your blog's content:

1. Hootsuite

Hootsuite is considered one of the best performing tools for Instagram users when it comes to scheduling as well as displaying and reporting on analytics. The application is known for keeping track of engagement numbers and audience data and statistics for Instagram accounts. The application will give you a detailed report on your blog's analytics–depending on the payment plan you sign up for.

For example, the tool is able to quantify sentiments and its tracking is so extensive it is able to track users' locations–this is great if you want to know where the majority of your followers are viewing your content from. You are able to see these detailed metrics as well as posts that contain terms (keywords, hashtags, etc.) that you are monitoring–on one dashboard--which makes viewing your information much easier. If you are struggling with tending to your customers/followers' questions, demands and orders, you can simply mark posts and delegate them to members of your team who will be able to handle the messages and responses for you.

The application offers a **free plan** as well as **other premium plans** with varying prices.

2. Brandwatch

Brandwatch is the perfect application to use if you want specific information on your target audience and the actual audience you are attracting. This platform is best when you want to analyze the audience you have managed to attract, and it will also size them up in relation to the audience you wish to harness as your followers and customers. This how the platform does it: it will track your audience's information such as age, gender, location, nationality (if available), interests and occupations. The platform will also make sure that you receive summarized and real-time alerts when users are talking about your brand online so that you are able to react to the posts quickly. Mega brands often use platforms like Brandwatch to monitor how their brands are discussed on social media so that they can handle any customer dissatisfaction as quickly as possible. The platform also makes community communication and management easier by filtering any content that may appear to be duplicated or spam.

If you are interested in working with Brandwatch, you can contact them through their site so that they can give you a unique plan (a plan tailored according to your brand, your audience and your needs).

3. AgoraPulse

AgoraPulse is one of the best platforms to use to publish Instagram posts while observing engagement and brand-related statistics. This tool takes note of Instagram users who share your content and the users who use your brand's hashtags and keywords; when this happens, the tool sends you notifications so that you can respond quickly and maintain engagement with these users. The platform also offers community management data, rate of response, for example, by tracking how long it takes you to react to users who mention your brand. This application also allows you to monitor your Instagram accounts (if you have multiple accounts) through one dashboard–this is a tool that's designed for social media managers and brands with multiple accounts, though.

The price range for this application is from $29 USD to $199 USD–depending on the plan you choose to sign up for.

4. Iconosquare

The dashboard on this platform contains analytics for the followers you have gained and the followers you have lost–this feature might have been affected by Instagram made a few changes that disabled the ability to track followers and unfollowers through third party applications. The tool also allows you to track your audience's location. The tool's greatest feature is the detailed data it produces through tracking hashtags that are relevant to your brand, including volume of activity and the level of influence the accounts that are posting hold. The tool offers to send you reports via email.

Plan prices range from $4.90—$49.90 USD per month for every Instagram account.

5. Quintly

Quintly is one of the top marketing tools social media users turn to; the tool allows you to measure your Instagram blog against your competitors' blogs.

The platform displays information on engagement from different accounts in the form of graphs–this allows you to easily measure performance and set goals and targets accordingly.

For example, if you are able to see how many shares you receive, in comparison to a number of your competitors, per post, you will be able to adjust your strategy accordingly. The tool also sends automated messages that will comprise of a detailed report of your Instagram account's data–you also get to choose which data should be included in the report. You can also choose when the tool should send you the reports and how often. The minimum plan price is $129 USD per month; the advanced plans differ.

6. SquareLovin

Squarelovin is the perfect application for someone with a low–to-non-existent budget and is only interested in seeing how their Instagram account is faring on the platform.

This tool displays follower growth in charts which are next to information on engagement; this information includes top posts (in terms of number of likes and the number of comments from followers). The tool also makes suggestions on how you can optimize your content, which will be based on the engagement your account receives. The tool will give you recommendations on the best filters to use, the types of hashtags you should use, as well as the best time for you to post.

The platform is free of charge, which makes it easy for new bloggers and bloggers who are on a tight budget to check their blog's statistics without trouble.

7. Unmetric

This is a more advanced–and expensive–platform tool to use; it's advisable that only experienced bloggers and established brands use this platform. One of this tool's strong points is that it will analyze your Instagram strategies against the strategies your competitors use.

The tool will give you the basic information, too–follower growth as well as engagement data. The tool will also gauge how influential your brand's voice is in relation to your competitors' by measuring the engagement and follower growth of your closest opposing brands. Unmetric will also give you a very detailed Microsoft Excel and Microsoft PowerPoint report–depending on the settings of your choice (frequency, detail, etc.) The tool is so extensive, it can provide you with up to four years of history (data) which will help you discover how well past strategies worked for you.

This advanced tool's pricing starts at $490 USD.

8. Keyhole

Keyhole allows you to track certain information from any public Instagram account, and it also allows you to track metrics revolving around specific hashtags and keywords.

The tool analyzes data like engagement and follower growth so that it can offer you accurate–and effective–suggestions for improving your account. For example, it will let you know when are the best times for you to post in order to boost your account's following and engagements.

When it comes to tracking hashtags and keywords, the platform will collect old *and* real-time metrics that are affiliated with your search terms. This will include organic and follower reach, impressions on your posts, and any related phrases, as well as the volume of activity around your Instagram blog. You can also get summarized information in emailed reports. Prices for this tool start at $89 USD.

9. Instagram Insights

If you aren't interested in using third party applications, you could always stick to Instagram's built-in analytics tool.

You will need to convert your profile to a business profile, first–which is a very easy and undemanding task. Once you have converted your profile, you will have access to information like impressions (number of times your post was viewed, liked and possibly shared), engagement and reach–these are metrics that measure the efficacy of your posts.

Instagram Insights are also able to provide follower statistics like the age, location and gender of your audience but this will only be specific to your account. You will not be able to measure your account's effectiveness against your competitors' effectiveness using Instagram Insights. This platform is free of charge.

Parting Words

The road to establishing your brand on Instagram is a long one, but it is filled with lessons and experiences that will help you become a better blogger, marketer and brand in the long haul. If you follow the advice and tips provided in this book, you will be able to see fruitful results with time.

We'll end this book off with a few reminders and words of advice to help you along the way:

- Always keep in mind what your brand is meant to be about and what it is meant to represent.

- Don't forget to stay consistent with your uploading, and remember to maintain a theme or aesthetic for your blog.

- Never let an external brand or financial contributor compromise your brand's image and reputation for financial gain.

- View your competitors as healthy competition and nothing else. Do not dedicate valuable time to stalking them and trying to gain the upper hand when you could be using that time to improve your brand.

- Always engage with your followers; don't see them as your fans, see them as a part of your community–see them as family.

- Give occasional shoutouts to fellow Instagram users; good gestures always go a long way.

- Never be afraid to think out of the box; the results could be outstanding.

- *Do not buy followers!*

- Lastly, when it seems like your blog is not making any progress, do not give up. Things are often tough before one is able to catch a break. Keep doing what you do, study your analytics, make sure your captions and hashtags are relevant and keep on pushing. It will work out in the end.

We wish you all the best with your journey to establishing your Instagram blog, and we look forward to sharing your blog as an example to aspiring brands and Instagram bloggers in the near future.

Get an Audio Book for FREE!

Don't have an Audible account?

Sign up and get "Instagram Marketing" audio book for FREE!

https://goo.gl/WaVpL8

One Last Thing... Did You Enjoy the Book?

If so, then let me know by leaving a review on Amazon! Reviews are the lifeblood of independent authors. I would appreciate even a few words from you!

If you did not like the book, then please tell me! Email me at lizard.publishing@gmail.com and let me know what you didn't like. Perhaps I can change it. In today's world a book doesn't have to be stagnant; it should be improved with time and feedback from readers like you. You can impact this book, and I welcome your feedback. Help me make this book better for everyone!

Printed in Great Britain
by Amazon